NEW POETRIES II

Also available from Carcanet

New Poetries

New Poetries II

an anthology

edited by Michael Schmidt

CARCANET

First published in 1999 by
Carcanet Press Limited
4th Floor, Conavon Court
12-16 Blackfriars Street
Manchester M3 5BQ

A CIP catalogue record for this book
is available from the British Library
ISBN 1 85754 349 1

The publisher acknowledges financial assistance
from the Arts Council of England

Set in 10pt Bembo by Bryan Williamson, Frome
Printed and bound in England by SRP Ltd, Exeter

CONTENTS

PREFACE

The cities in Jeremy Over's and Stephen Burt's poems are very different places; the political worlds which Monica Youn and Karen Press address could hardly be more remote from one another. Yet this anthology, more than *New Poetries I*, suggests significant common ground. The poets are gathered from the four corners of the English-speaking world and each has a distinct voice, yet all are available, in their complex difference of accent, culture and landscape, to any English-speaking readership. Even those poems most coloured by a specific locality and its politics are poems first, statements afterwards. They say something, but before they speak fully, they *do* something in rhythm, diction, form.

The writers featured in *New Poetries II* are not unknown. Of the baker's dozen, Karen Press and Emma Lew have published books in their own countries (South Africa and Australia). Sinéad Morrissey has published a collection with Carcanet: she is here because she *ought* to have been in *New Poetries I* and because her recent work – especially that written during her years in Japan – marks a fascinating change from the poetry of *There Was Fire in Vancouver*.

Monica Youn, Nicole Krauss and Stephen Burt have begun making names for themselves as poets and critics in the United States where they live, and in Britain where they were students a couple of years ago. Other poets here were their contemporaries at university. Most of these writers are not yet – or not quite – thirty; all have contributed to *PN Review*.

We are far from the vague realm of the post-Modern (only Jeremy Over, Patrick Mackie and Matthew Welton might at first seem to be approaching us from that indirection); it is, however, a realm in which formal choices have been made and stuck to. With poetry the formal challenges and solutions are the durable element, unfashionable though it may be to say so. In this anthology readers will find much that should prove durable, elements of what in the introduction to *New Poetries I* was called 'the something more than promise' of the poets included.

I am surprised once more to note the impact of Wallace Stevens on several of these writers: Stevens himself, not Stevens via Ashbery (though Ashbery has a place in their firmament); and Stevens, not Pound. It is as though Ezra Pound's Modernism has yet to brush the wings of those poets who know the East, and as if Eliot's influence is oblique, mediated through other writers – Joseph Brodsky, perhaps, or Randall Jarrell. Auden is not near at hand here. This *fin-de-siècle*, in some of its manifestations, seems as enchanted by subtle prosodies as the last.

Like any good anthology of new poems, this is a book of surprises. Pastoral clouds will float across urban suns, turning tenement or skyscraper shadows wonderfully green. Jeremy Over's huge cornucopia of images spills out pineapples, watermelons; he dares to glance down from vertiginous perspectives and the laughter his poems produce is bright and innocent. There is nothing reductive in his ironies. He leans upon Neruda but readers will feel in his work the pressure of the Lorca of *Poeta en Nueva York* and the tonalities of Laforgue. Stephen Burt, an intense heir of Randall Jarrell and one of the briskest-minded critics of his generation, shares his poetic energies and anxieties with a Spanish original, too, Jaime Gil de Biedma, inventively collaborating to make the worlds of his own poems. Nicole Krauss shapes narratives and verse essays out of lives and works of art, setting herself appropriately demanding formal challenges. With Matthew Welton and Patrick Mackie, rhythm and word-play deliver up worlds as arranged, deepened and enchanted as those of Stevens, and as rewardingly 'real'. Love finds its paradoxes in Caroline Sylge's and Patrick McGuinness's writing (they have other themes as well); and a rural bias makes Oliver Marlow's scenes at once haunted and familiar.

Passion and play abound. Both can become appallingly serious, as in Monica Youn's 'The Scythian Lamb'; or political when a poet is finding appropriate speech for a radically changing culture (as Karen Press and Sinéad Morrissey are); or classically elegiac as in some of Emma Lew's poems.

There is an abundance of *world* in this book. An aural world of voices and accents, each inflected and formally realised in an appropriate prosody, is to be discovered here. There are also the worlds of culture, politics, landscape and the specific worlds of love and loss out of which the imaginations of these thirteen poets are made. As in *New Poetries I* a sufficient selection of each writer's work is presented so that readers can take more than a casual measure of the poets. Even when their tones are most casual, these poets have expectations of the reader at least as great as the reader has of them.

Michael Schmidt

Matthew Welton

The Wonderment of Fundament

In Germany the weather hasn't changed.
The concert-room is peppishness unhinged.

Tonight the lady pianist who plays
con fuoco hardly hears her own applause.

*

A Mr Macaroni stops his Ford
two streets away and lets the engine flood,

the radio just loud enough to hear,
one crate of pippin-apples, one of beer.

*

She makes her music, loosening her hands:
the moment holds. But if the evening ends

the coffee place will crowd, and trains will leave,
and fields absorb what light the moon might give.

*

These city birds among these city trees
sing slow above this greyness in the grass,

and Mr Macaroni pours his beer
and rattles apples up against his ear.

Springtime

She only lives a street or two away.
Still everyday there's something in the mail.

A picture-card without too much to say,
just where she's been and who she's seen, that's all.

She never telephones or comes around.
This morning where the postman left his bike

the shadow that it spread along the ground
was hardly there, and no one was awake.

Two Hands

Noon
The dizzy girl walked quickly down the beach.

1.05
The roads were slow. The fields were full of fruit.
The smiling boy drove up beside the beach.

2.11
The landlord turned the lightswitch on the wall.
The room was dark, and smelled of winter fruit.
They pulled the shade and watched the empty beach.

3.16
She spoke his name and walked across the room
and did him quickly up against the wall.
They lit cigarettes. They shared a piece of fruit.
He talked. She stared outside, towards the beach.

4.22
The bulky policeman made his usual rounds –
the dairy yard, the parks, the snooker rooms.
He turned and crossed towards the warehouse walls,
the market stands, the yellow fish, the fruit.
He took the quick way back, along the beach.

5.27
He talked about a place they used to know –
his smile got dim, her eyes became less round –
his cousin's house a mile from here, the rooms
he'd decorate each spring, the garden walls,
the ponds with frogs, the yard that stank like fruit,
the fires they'd make with driftwood from the beach.

6.33
She told him as she leaned against the stairs
it's not the only house she's ever known.
She talked about a street where friends came round,
an orchestra, a city where her room
was clean and cheap, with nothing on the walls.
And coming home, her face as bruised as fruit.
And pacing down the beach. The bastard beach.

7.38
For him these furnished evenings never match
that kick, that itch, of shuffling up the stairs
and listening for some voice you think you know,
of knocking once, then twice, then slipping round
the back, of chasing through the basement rooms,
of forcing doors, of slamming into walls,
of striking matches, crouched in crates of fruit,
of watching from the warehouse by the beach.

8.43
The room grew darker. Cars went by outside.
For everything that's wrong, he struck a match:
that ugly mary coming up the stairs,
the radio with songs you think you know,
the tenants' goosey daughters hanging round,
the syrup-marmalade, the breakfast room,

the landlord with a glass against the wall,
the typing-paper bedsheets, polished fruit,
the photographs of donkeys on the beach.

9.49
A panda car drew up across the street.
The bars were full, with people stood outside.
The moon was slim, and dimmer than a match,
and while the smiling boy raced down the stairs
and dogged about as if he didn't know
the road from here, the ambulance pulled round
the front and stopped outside the Chestnut Rooms.
He carried on and waited by the wall
then kicked his way among the rinds of fruit
that washed along the edges of the beach.

10.54
She caught her own reflection in the glass
and stopped a moment, staring at the street.
She sat and smoked. A light came on outside.
She crossed her legs. She lit a kitchen match.
She swore out loud. She shouted down the stairs,
and rattled off about some girl she knew.
She spent a moment sparrowing around
with coins and clothes and cases through the room.
She hung a pocket mirror on the wall
and hacked her hair, and finished up the fruit.
She left, and pounded down the muddy beach.

Midnight
She hurried past the promenade, the pier,
and joined him in the café for a glass
of milk. He took her arm and crossed the street
and put her in a cab. He stepped inside
the boarding house. He tried to get a match
to light. He slumped off down the cellar stairs.

The road was blocked. The driver said he knew
a quicker way and turned the taxi round.

The landlord found the policeman in the room
behind the snooker club. He thumped the wall
until his hands were raw and ripe, like fruit.
He took the slow way back, along the beach.

Butternuts

The girl who smelled like bubblegum admired the sky.
The telephone rang loudly. Moss grew on the roof.
The neighbours from across the lake would straggle by
for parties in the winter. Pairs of girls would goof

around the gardens where the paths were pebbled green.
The gummy girl would hardly talk. The night it rained
she danced a hula, fingering a tangerine.
She showed her teeth. *The sky is faultless*, she explained.

★

The drunken uncles glooped around the garden-house
then went indoors and offered round their loose cigarettes
and hammered out some practice-piece and sang like cows.
The grey canary-gulls, they said, they kept as pets.

At night the smell of apricot would drowse the rooms.
But now the radio comes on and plays some march
with scrawly cellos, gasps of organ, piles of drums.
The trays of seedlings flourish in the kitchen porch.

★

All night they talked of breakfast. When the morning came
they cut the meat which tasted more like swedes, or beer.
The bony man with monkey-teeth was blue as blame,
as caned as custard, juiced as jellied-eels. But here

the air takes on a taste of kaolin, or yeast,
or starch, or lemon-leaf. The evenings drop like plums.
As spruced as sprouts. As waxed as wasps. Completely spliced.
The breezes soften. Rain comes down. The heating hums.

*

The upstairs smelled of biro ink. The kitchen smelled
like rained-on wool. The gardens smelled like boiling milk.
The wind that blew blew slowly, and the circuits failed.
The rug was rashed with sun. The dark-faced girl would walk

about the bright and rainy streets. She peeled a pear.
The cousins in the kitchen played their reel of tape:
an hour's recorded silence. Shirts hung on a chair.
The sky was deep, and soft. The sky was chocolate soup.

*

The clouds collapse like coals. The sausage-dog that ate
the pears collapses by the trees, then comes inside.
The phone rang loudly. Papers blackened in the grate.
She answered *Yes. A moment, please* – and walked outside

and swam around the lake. The gardens smelled like tin.
A smudge of sun, a whiff of wind; the rain that falls
falls early in the day. The afternoon wears in.
The shadow shifts in sheets, and daylight blues the walls.

Sometimes I see me dead in the rain

Ecclesiastes Malin at the hills behind the house.
Ecclesiastes Malin in the river. Treading mud.
Talking through his teeth. At day, laying out the whittleknife.
Returning from the lower rooms with sugar on his breath.

Ecclesiastes Malin with that look that leaves his face
resembling something scorched, or something strained, or something soured.
And as it comes to darkness, whispering quickly to himself.
Ecclesiastes Malin with his fist inside his mouth.

★

The way the morning brings the wind that smells like berryfruit.
Those goatbones in the yard. The little scale of blackbirdsong.
A greenness to this light. A slowness to the evening wind
that stirs the clouds. The sun across his face, at night the moon.

These dawns and noons, these dusks that come. The simple falls of night.
The millpool and its minnowfish. The dusts the noontimes bring.
These apples hung above the stream. The hackknife in his hand.
The wind all night. Ecclesiastes nowhere to be seen.

★

Ecclesiastes Malin with his fingers in this tree
whose branches lend their shadows down the paths across the fields,
that buds and leafs, growing a fruit that smells like fruit gone bad.
This sense of evening settled in the woods along the hill.

And smoke that rises. Rain that falls. This wind that dries the air.
These things that bring Ecclesiastes silent to these roads,
across this sunned-in square, beneath the turning weatherbird.
These things that see Ecclesiastes whistling at the wall.

★

The woods acquiring darkness as his bones take on the cold,
the way the morning takes its dampness from the dwindled night.
The summer has him moving slowly, spitting like a hen.
The summer has him waking in the drying heathergrass.

The winds that breeze above the stream. The streams that cut the field.
Tickling grayling. Eyeing the sun. Untethering a boat.
Ecclesiastes chewing chalk. A greyness to the rain.
And furrowed cloud. And birdcall in the night. And littler stars.

London Sundays

Snatches of summer in afternoon parks
are probably now as good as it gets.
Meeting beneath the clock that never works
then sloping off homewards as the sun sets
behind the band-stand must be the closest
anyone can come to finding again
that good good feeling that will last and last
like a child's holidays. Dusk comes. Then rain.

And love never really feels like some craze
that hits like gin, buzzes like benzedrine,
and smells as good as coffee. In some ways
all it has to be is something between
a half-funny joke and some old rumour
from somewhere around, that arrives unrushed
like boredom, wears on like a bad winter,
and which spreads through rooms like sunlight and dust.

President Marbles

Or the Wednesday morning, or the orange-lime rinds,
or the frog-fish, or the fiver folded lengthways,
or the puffball mushrooms, or the silent house-guests,
or the fractured lightbulb, or the cornflakes with cream.

Or the sturdy, sturdy girl with the folded hands,
or the chicory-cheese, or the short avenues,
or the puddle-mud, or the children with fat wrists,
or the pint of tea, or the large pineapple farm.

Or, in the dusk-brown dip of evening, skanking off
by the perch-ponds, or holing up at the fives-hall.
The shirt-paper. The gimbal-stove. The duff-pastry.
The juniper-juice. Or, alone here in the road,

the goony girl, the gusty girl, the huffy guff.
The gumptious girl. That total gaggle of a girl.
The gummy girl. The gloomy girl. The hickory.
The limb-loose girl with teeth like nuts. That pebblehead.

Or the dead-dozen daisy-pans. The wrap of zap.
The little muff of roll-your-own. Or those crew-necks.
Or the chicken-shit father, the chicken-shit son.
The tree on the square. This woman who wouldn't kiss.

The you-are-here map. The penny-slot telescope.
The sheet-music. The chocolate-box instamatics.
These breakfast-plates. That photograph signed with crayon.
The room with the willow-wood chair. This lightlessness.

The Fundament of Wonderment

She said her name was little jones
and bended back her fingerbones

and sang a song in minor thirds.
She spilled a smile and spoke her words.

★

Up here the river turns its boats.
She brings out books of pencil-notes,

her letters from, her letters to,
her clarkesville park, her london zoo.

★

And, in the wind and where she walks
above the blue nasturtium stalks

at london zoo, the smells of apes
are like the smells of table grapes.

*

The mice and monkeys tell the trees
the wind will end, the worlds will freeze.

She moves herself beyond the grass
the blue boats pass. The blue boats pass.

Monica Youn

A Parking Lot in West Houston

Angels are unthinkable
in hot weather

except in some tropical locales where,
from time to time, the women catch one in their nets

hang it to dry, and fashion it into a lantern
that will burn forever on its own inexhaustible oils.

But here – shins smocked with heat rash,
the supersaturated air. We no longer believe

in energies pure enough not to carry heat,
nor in connections – the thought of someone

somewhere warming the air we breathe
that one degree more . . .

In a packed pub during the World Cup final,
a bony redhead woman gripped my arm

too hard. *I could see how a bloke might fancy you.*
Like a child's perfect outline in fast-melting snow,

her wet handprint on my skin, disappearing.
The crowd boiling over, a steam jet: *Brrra-zil!*

And Paris – a heroin addict
in the basement of the Pompidou Center

who put her hypodermic to my throat:
Je suis malade. J'ai besoin de medicaments.

Grabbing her wrist, I saw
her forearm's tight net sleeve of drying blood.

I don't like to be touched.
I stand in this mammoth parking lot,

car doors open, letting the air conditioner
run for a while before getting in.

The heat presses down equally
everywhere. It wants to focus itself,

to vaporise something instantaneously,
efficiently – that shopping cart, maybe,

or that half-crushed brown glass bottle –
but can't quite. Asphalt softens in the sun.

Nothing's detachable.
The silvery zigzag line

stitching the tarmac to the sky around the edges
is no breeze, just a trick of heat.

My splayed-out compact car half-sunk
in the tar pit of its own shadow

strong-shouldered, straining to raise
its stunted vestigial wings.

The Scythian Lamb

1

How was myopic Sir John
of Mandeville to know
that what he glimpsed on the far bank

of the monsoon-fed Kabul
was but a hapless *Cibotium barometz*,
rudely tossed, fronds down, roots up,

by a badger in hot pursuit
of a frantic, wide-eyed
white-footed mouse.

It grew dark early at that time of year,
and, too, his reading public
was hungry for more living logs,

river horses, and rabbits in plate armour
with the faces of Christian martyrs –
anything to keep their minds

off the Black Death.
The travellers stopped, made camp.
Sir John shook out his pen.

'In the wilds of Scythia,'
he wrote, 'there grows
a wondrous and woolly thing

half-beast, half-vegetable,
a lambkin on a stalk.'
He paused, looked out again

over the darkening
Afghan river. 'Its cloven hooves
cannot reach ground;

for sustenance, it munches
those grasses within its reach.'
Sir John moved closer to the fire.

'When this fails, as it must,
the Scythian lamb will wither.
The wind carries its seeds

to more fertile soil, leaving only
a dried-up stalk, a circle
of close-cropped earth.'

2

In February, in Fort Worth
before the headlines started screaming,
ten-year-old Douglas Hill

tried to make no noise
as he went down the basement stairs
to get a beer for his father.

He tiptoed across the concrete floor
toward the refrigerator,
averting his eyes from the opposite wall

where his older brother Stephen
(now at sixty pounds)
sat chained to a pipe in the corner.

Douglas risked a look back . . .
then grabbed the beer and ran,
footsteps thudding up the stairs,

the refrigerator slamming shut,
as he tried to clear his mind
of the sight of his brother:

dull-eyed, quiescent,
jaws working methodically
on a mouthful that wasn't there.

Night Ferry to Naxos 1

All your carefully cultivated notions of realism

come to an end here, where the sentimental pink
funnels into the Peloponnese

like a rum and grenadine cocktail
poured down a taut throat. Tourist,

this is how the peace drains into you.
Your fingers uncurl on the deck railings,

and over your head, a spiralling umbilical
of ship-smoke loops back to the brown air of Athens,

which only now, behind you, is beginning
to take shape: a huddled, smog-shielded dome.

The flattering breeze picks out your contours
in silverpoint – its insinuations

sweet as fresh-laid sheets, a bed-time story,
mother-love. Already above you,

half-heard, a tattoo of wingbeats, bare feet
racing in circles on hard-packed dirt.

You will have to become a hero like the rest of us.

Night Ferry to Naxos 2

Another round of *Dona Nobis Pacem*

from the Italian ladies below deck and you know
you'll never be rid of it now.

You're still humming *sotto voce* at 3 a.m.
when a wall of the warm hold opens up

on the blank dark and, still souvenir-sized,
this island, coy as a cameo

on a dowager's black bosom. You step,
wind-whipped and hugging yourself,

onto the gangplank. Everything
is ready. Since April, a honeyed

habit-forming dew has been collecting
in the hollows of the rocks,

and the local myths, freshly washed,
have been polishing their bare limbs.

Fingernails frescoed with whitewash,
mouths gritty with waterfront coffee,

the dock hawks are closing in. All awaits
your melodramatic approach: the *deus*

ex machina in silver lamé
a lobster on an enormous plate, a birth . . .

Nothing you can do will disappoint them now.

Stealing *The Scream*

It was hardly a high-tech operation, stealing *The Scream*.
That we know for certain, and what was left behind –
a store-bought ladder, a broken window,
and fifty-one seconds of videotape, abstract as an overture.

And the rest? We don't know. But we can envision
moonlight coming in through the broken window,
casting a bright shape over everything: the paintings,
the floor tiles, the velvet ropes — a single, sharp-edged pattern;

the figure's fixed hysteria turned suddenly ironic
by the fact of something happening;
houses clapping a thousand shingle hands to shocked cheeks
along the road from Oslo to Asgardstrand;

the guards rushing in — too late — greeted only
by the gap-toothed smirk of the museum walls;
and dangling from the picture wire like a baited hook,
a postcard print: 'Thanks for the poor security.'

The policemen, lost as tourists, stand whispering in the gallery,
    '. . . but what does it all mean?'
Someone has the answers, someone who, grasping the frame, saw his
    own face
        reflected, sun-red, in that familiar boiling sky.

St Benedict's Painted Church
Honaunau, Kona

Something, a fruit perhaps,
or a bowl of fruit —
something collapsed

in upon itself,
collapsed in on itself
again and again till it rose

in packed banks, layer
upon layer, a carnival-
coloured amphitheatre.

But it can't have been like that,
as I remembered it. I've lost
both postcards,

my notebook: *a man upright*
in the tomb rays of light
threaded through his palms

a sainted marionette . . .
the devils wear braided pigtails . . .
the fig tree trunks are spiralling

scrolls spiralling praise him. . . .
No, it would be better to start
from the beginning, the outside:

a green hill rising
out of an island
rising out of the sea.

Then nearer, it is peaked,
foursquare: the marvellous
origami husband-

hunting machines we folded
out of hymn sheets
during Children's Mass –

shuffling once, twice,
forty times, then lifting a flap
to reveal a name.

And finally, so melodramatically
the gravel bursts into applause
as we skid to a stop on the driveway,

it's there: clapboarded, so much
in earnest, the sunlight
hung out to dry on its pitched roof.

We step inside, into that shaped
impenetrable space *as if*
a seed had sprouted

while still inside the shell.
Louder outside now the slow ticking
of the actual vegetation.

Mrs Caldwell Speaks to her Son: The Young Filmmaker

Last night, my son, we attended a special lecture
delivered by an 18-year-old lesbian filmmaker
who had given a one-woman show at the Whitney.

She was from Milwaukee (it was evident
in her wide-spaced dishwater eyes,
in the shallow blemishes on her pale, thick cheeks).
There clung to her something of the breweries,
it was if her chin and fingertips had been saturated
with the yeasty, exhausted smell of the breweries.

She said her short film clips told the story
of a kind of evolution (she wasn't very clear).
She never once mentioned Milwaukee.

Despite my best intentions, I must admit
my mind drifted. I thought of you first,
then found myself recalling
that unfortunate woman at the New Year's Ball
(I'm sure I must have told you about her)
dancing so vigorously in her boned bodice
before falling completely out of it.

And she kept on – her eyes bulging out
and glazed over like cheap earthenware;
her mouth hanging open as she panted for breath,
for all the world like a colicky infant.

(You, my dear, were never afflicted with the colic.
You were, if anything, too still as a baby,
displaying your fragile blue veins with all the artistry
of those admirable Elizabethan ladies,
who touched up their wrists with cobalt
to highlight the pathways leading
to their warm hearts, their indelicate hearts.)

As a spectacle she was an utter failure;
no one was even amused.
We all averted our eyes, of course,
but some of us let our mouths gape open
slightly, as if by accident.

Perhaps it wasn't necessary for you
to have watched these events yourself.
You can see them as well
through my eyes as through your own.
Too much detail, I fear,
would only distract you.

But how can I assure myself
that you have grasped
with the proper acumen,
what is truly important
in these two brief episodes?

What an opportunity to witness,
within a few short months,
two separate epiphanies! (a word
one sees so rarely in the plural).
That unfortunate woman,
her sheen of sweat suddenly cold
on her forehead and upper lip,
as she looked down.

And that young filmmaker girl – all at once
coarser, more awkward, as she retracted
that earlier statement she had immortalised
with her forty-dollar plastic camera:
'At least I'm not a midget;
at least I'm not a bearded lady.'

Caroline Sylge

Egyptian Cotton

Somewhere
Your upper arm
Lies against a sheet
Me on one side of you.

Elsewhere
My ankle bone
Touches the news page
Of a Sunday paper.
In Egyptian cotton trousers
I am eating a hot-cross bun.

Striped cloth
Encasing legs
Is our soft white sheet.
My fresh-aired eyes blink at the print,
Small black currants on my pink tongue.

Somewhere
Elsewhere
Friends go out to meet.

Climbing

The men were graceless, the women too,
Climbing up to the mountain.
Helly hansons, hiking boots,
Hair blowing out about them.

The sun had put rays on the valley:
Look how beautiful I am.
But fog came out of ginger,
Thoughts of safety got them down.

If we could get on top of mountains,
I would climb with you to the massive sky.
What is it now that trembles about me
Stopping my eye?

There is here a piece of emptying space
Something like fear takes us to.
After, we give names to namelessness:
Twenty miles, hailstones, soaked toes.

No one behaves in the way you want,
Not even you can reach a state of grace.
I sit on top of a nondescript hill
To watch your face.

Battista's .

From a café across the street
I see you walking.

My eye once fixed now shifts
But I make no move.
I follow you from left to right
Your thoughts on the pavement.

At the tops of the buildings
Dotted on the steps of the bus
Jigging the air
A lie is at work.
You silent
In your collarless shirt.
One of the rest.

Angel

As I grow up I realise
It is not love that gives me the ache,
To be somewhere clean and cool
Like a meadow in shadow.
My mother says I would be perfect if I stopped my smoking,
But she doesn't know the half of it.

After a tired day I can still smile,
Go to Tesco Express to buy humus and lettuce leaves,
Laugh loud into a good book.
But on the way home tonight
Nearing Angel on the 38
The wind shook and I heard the trees.

The Potato Café

Fairy liquid niggles the knives in the sink,
Car ads filter the room with cigarette smoke,
A tourist shuffles in, fingering a map.

Peering over his glasses at the menu board,
Gourmet Mr Hicks spots a ham-and-cheese-filled bap.

Steppo brings an expresso to a chipboard table,
A Suit selects a styrofoam cup of tomato,
Sally leaves, brushing dog hair from her second hand coat.

You say something irrelevant, I a husky titter.
The inside of my cup is a mud bath bittering my throat.

Outside plastic chairs scrape noisily on the pavement,
A fat man with a high wife is ordering a steak,
Chips wrestle with the whiff of a green English salad.

I am plastered on the mayonnaise I stir with my fork.
Your food arrives, you start to eat to your own silent ballad.

It is not love I want to talk about,
Though the waitress steadily watches us
And a tired and honest corner couple
Are waiting for the memory to come back.

Wearing Gloves in Brahms and Liszt

Intrinsic
Sightly
Leather-dressed,
Your eye rests on the
Tiny black thread seams
Holding my fingers together.

I scurry with my scarf,
You watch thumb pads
Move grey silk into knots.

Inside
Life lines sweat,
Blue veins match
Bruises
Won in a hazy state.

Black covers off, your skin
Puts pressure on silver rings
And squeezes.

Nothing is said.
Not even the air knows,
How fast my fingers scurry,
How far my hands will reach.

John Redmond

St MacDara's Island

Two men might float a cow to Mweenish
in a slapdash currach on a slow, calm day
but even the Twelve Disciples, God knows,
would have been damn glad to get out alive,

as these trippers from the looming ferry
with their high-strung boots and rucksacks
leaped on to our boat ('Watch my foot!')
and we got lower and lower in the water.

Leaning towards me in your denim jacket,
you shouted, 'I can't swim. It's getting in.'
And it was true: the Atlantic lifted its smooth face
high, slurping, licking, like some monster

to be caressed and I murmured, 'It's okay. Okay',
as the island rose and fell with its church
and hands stretched out from the other ferry.
The panic, I saw, had brought your face alive.

Everyone got off again. You first. Me last
as, slow to move, I made like a castaway
turning to driftwood – a gazing mood
the others guessed was shock. Much later,
as I wiped the wet hair out of your eyes,
you asked what I'd been thinking about,

and I said, 'a church the size of a small boat.'

Perhaps Then

Perhaps the sun now shudders and goes down
one island further along.
Perhaps the sea remembers its shawl
one inch higher up the sea-wall.
Perhaps the big spheres in the early grasses
the beads of sweat on gravestone faces

swoop fractionally faster to Earth.
Perhaps no one goes in to Seán's bar anymore.
Perhaps Mac has had it up to here

with abalones, with the TV thumping,
with a brother who can't hear his own swallow.
Perhaps the band in O'Rourke's has learnt how to play.

Perhaps Máirtín has scoured all the scurf off his boat
and Cha, in ramming it, ramming it home,
no longer shouts 'it's a gooo-al!'
Perhaps Dundass has taken his son by the throat.

Perhaps Taig is no longer quite Taigeen
and his parents no longer mention heaven
and where the rusty gate hangs on to its indecision
perhaps Lemass has compressed his whole fortune

into an Eden of crag and nettle.
Perhaps the world no longer stops at Jack's gate
and strolls out of town by a different route
and the ass has stepped from its long-standing mound
and the trees by the stream make a lazier sound.

Perhaps the houses at night flicker
                                    rather than shine
and the car-lights move in an unbroken line.

Perhaps they have forgotten.

Or where window sweeps and car skids in
where shore gleams and shirt buttons down

where dog spills, cloud cools and pub steams
where pier clicks, boat leans, wheel buckles and wire hums,
perhaps nothing at all has changed.

Perhaps then you will stay.

Feenish Island

You cannot walk to an island unless,
at low tide, it is not an island.
You cannot leave the mainland
unless the mainland is already an island.
Europe is part of an island. Ireland,
an island, is part of Europe. The Irish for island
is *inis* and the island of Feenish is Irish.
Ireland is islands.
                          Europe is Irelands.
The blue-green globe on the ormolu console
glitters with the pergola's inclusive glow.
The cool niche of the Chinoiserie bridge,
the fountain of inches, the shiny rosy-trellis,
the blue tiles glowing in diamonds and squares
are almost still in the infinite breeze.

The cows hide their heads behind their bodies,
as if the wind had cut their throats.
The heron swivels his bill to Mweenish.
You cannot find a roof between the gables.
You cannot find a floor between the walls.
You cannot see your shoes, deep in the sand,

but you can feel them twist in the rabbit-holes.
You cannot open a door but you can walk
through empty door-frames. You cannot get out
of the wind, unless you get off the island.
You cannot see the islanders, they are long gone,

but you can enter the islanders' houses,
the beachheads of their living-rooms,
and you can meet the persistent spray
entering one window after another.

The Gazing Ass

And though I had no time I slowed the car,
for a sleepy ass had stolen my road,
dipping his tail in an hourglass of legs.
A ewe would run, a cow would lumber away,
but, rather than bolt, as I drew close,
his nostrils grew broad, his ears grew high,
and he stared at me like there was nothing else.
Why was he waiting? What had I done?
Changing down to the side, I saw
his gaze was fixed like the gaze of my car,
for he kept on staring at where I had been.
He had not been looking at what he had seen.

In the Shadow of the House

Where there were two houses with two shadows,
there is one house and one house-shadow.

Where the ten-inch hope was transplanted,
a twenty-foot palm-tree splutters and sprawls.

Where a snarl of nettles scrapped with the wind,
our spades rip wetly out of the earth.

Where two wifeless tumbledown brothers
grew slowly to sideburns and madness

as they fished each day from a downstairs window,
(the same glassless window our childhood climbed through)

I look out at the wind in the sweep of the waves
and I watch a seagull repeatedly
bounce backwards in mid-air

and now — can you believe it? —
gravel flung down — after how many years? —
snapping across a longer, darker path,
and our spades pummelling the gravel-pile
to expose the shoulders of some sleeping thought.

Where I move across the winding, new path,
my shadow pulls itself to me.

Where a goosepimpled boy stayed out of the sun,
I pull myself out of the shadow.

Charlie and Joe

Why was Charlie Charlie and Joe Joe?
And why did we call the road west the road west
when we drove east on it as much as west?
Perhaps with all its islands and sunshowers
the western side of Ireland so enlarged us
it drew the eastern into itself until east
was a part of west — the eastern part of west
like they say that Earth is part of God
but God is more Himself elsewhere.
And the road itself? Why was it most itself
at night, when the landscape around it shivered off
into a starscape, when mingled with the stars
were planes, planets, streetlamps and satellites?
As 'cat's eyes' down the middle of the road
blinked over and over in white and gold
smoothly dividing the blaze of headlights

from the milder glow of crimson taillights,
my brother and I would fight on the back seat
to divide ourselves with an invisible line.
Father watched us in the rear-view mirror,
Mother flicked open her vanity-glass
and the little zodiac dashboard glowed.

Our hatchback, true, was not a full-fledged starship,
our back-seat, true, was not a hi-tech cockpit,
but from inside the Volkswagen we could see
the same outer space as any space-pilot.
And when, like stars coming down to our level,
the headlights of any oncoming car
would calmly return our open-faced stare,
and shortly come back for another look,
we would always call them Charlie and Joe.
Any names would have done but our own,
for we believed they were just like us:
two brothers, separate but inseparable,
who always went everywhere together.

And when they had gone and left us alone
our arms would widen, our hands would open
and we settled down to hugging the road
with weightless, imagined steering-wheels.
The Milky Way would sway from left to right,
as our hands flashed through the higher gears;
what we saw, we thought; what we thought,
we saw. For say the car was veering towards
a luminous sign for crossing deer,
then a deer was sure to leap from behind it.
Say a torch was flashed by the side of the road
it was surely related to Charlie and Joe.
And say we saw a red shape in the sky
slowly somersaulting through its trail of sparks –
as we did one journey near Ballinasloe –
then it was the vast mothership from *Close Encounters*,
not our mother letting a cigarette go.

Before And After

After murder, the sleep of murder,
its slipways closed, its map unclimbable.
But, before that, as a car-door flicks

into last year's Festival, it's early yet.
After a lock clicks, the car relaxes,
reflections flicker from shop to shop

and most of what he is hangs from his hand.
After a balloon, the weight of a child
unbalances him and something draws

against a hard corner – but before this –
ice cream, bells, a landscape of heifers,
mothers leaning across sunlit windshields

and, from side to side, nowhere to park,
except where bicycles curve their shadows
on separate outlines in the grass.

Before pickups crash across back fields,
there are small cries in the finishing trees.
Before the short flash of a coffinplate,

the scarecrow falls from an empty hat,
the sun twists through the country stiles,
the earthworms dive and rise and dive,

because what could be done had to be done.
After the town stands for the hearing,
before any sentence is read,

the newspaper shows two photographs:
This is his face as a young man.
And this is the man's face after.

Aurora

As the star that puts out other stars
by being close to us
has gone out, I guess, hours ago,
the wind that puts out other winds

by being visible –
this violently swivelling, turquoise wind –
has put me out of the house
like an early armchair astronomer.

Lowering my binoculars I find
two dark heads where my eyes were –
each haloed by sunflares,
the image of two far-gone Magi
which I, a doubting third,
follow at a distance,
behind the mirage they may have followed
by following a star.

Daumenbreite

'*Pancakes?* You really say peace, joy and *pancakes?*'
'Yes. *Friede, Freude, Eierküchen.*'
'And what's that word I like for water . . . ?'
Across the Shannon river, the train
reaches with another translation.
'We call freshwater sweetwater. *Süßwasser.*'
As she slowly unzips her bag
I touch a sugarcube to my coffee
and watch it soak up the river.
High, white girders of the bridge wheel by
as she leans to me with 'part of a wall':
a concrete knuckle wrapped in plastic.
'I knew you wouldn't get over it.
Everyone wants a piece of the Wall.'

We draw in to Galway station, laughing:
'I didn't think you would give me an inch.'
'Well, since we use metric, I didn't.' ('Inch'
and *Zentimeter* being miles apart.)

'Then give me something close to English measures.'
'How about *Daumenbreite* . . . ?'
'How big is that?'

She takes my thumb between two fingers.

We narrow it down to what is between us.

Karen Press

Application for naturalisation

Country.
Could your mountainous days ever fold around my arrival?
I wait in a room with blank walls that wait.
I go out among the sea, the streets, the sky:
they are too busy to make conversation.

Country:
must I become dust for your moonlight to drink?
You don't open my window.
I lean against the glass,
I hear you talking to the gulls all night.

I am luminous, not transparent,
a spell waiting to be uttered.
Country, become my shadow,
I will become your body.

I who live here, it is I

'This earth was the first to speak.
I have been pronounced once and for all.'
— Breyten Breytenbach, *Return to Paradise*

I

In my sleep I return here.

★

Being here, giving birth to my city I am
day by day being home, day by day
it has no name, seeds came from all parts of the known world
to plant me here, being myself these rooms, streets, rain, tides,
the air tasting of me, cool mist my hair, my skin hot stone,
the pulsing of hands my hands growing sand and wood
as the sky enters my eyes and the sea wells from my feet
and I turning inside out disappear into all manner of joyous bird cries
and the weeping of engines and wind,
gulls and avid rats feed where I feed,
consuming this limitless home swelling inside me
as I inside it open wide enough to die.

★

Coming home I see it coming towards me,
rubbing against me like a welcoming cat.

In my sleep I feel it leaning against me, sleeping.

★

Dried apricots, soft and sour
dawn wind stings the palm tree.

Neon rivers spilling across
the smell of buses pushing homeward.

★

In my sleep I return here.

II

It is only one look, one acrid glance shearing across the sweet blue hour
and the air pulls back, embarrassed at its intimacy,
leaving me naked as a captured slave, a trespasser, a thief.

All people ask: what are you doing here? what are you?
Eyes and eyes and eyes, scraping my shadow off all surfaces.

Any person here rebukes me.
Any person here in the streets of my home rebukes me.
I, walking like a strange person in the streets of my home
stare at my footsteps spread out on the road and deny them.
Any person is more at home here than I am.

The walls and the wind withdraw obediently from my skin.
I breathe in the bitter juice of any person looking at me,
peeling me off the air, expelling me.

All people live in my home and say it is not me, it is not,
all people invite me in and say look, it is not yours, welcome.

Any person has permission because of history.
Because of justice. Because of songs of genesis.
Any person being decidedly here in my self
banishes me. Any person refuses permission.
Any person who says nothing, or everything,
does not say my name. Any person is here in my place,
it is not my place.

How is it that my born home
is loyal to anyone who passes
in the street, following him like a hot beast
eager for better origins?

III

They say if my name were found here
buried in rock older and older
than any home a person can recall,
my home would return to me.

But no name is my home.
I am spread wider over the sand
than the width of a name.
Being born here the cells of my skin
are all the time of history.

What voice could pronounce the whole tide of my days?
What eyes could pour sky into my sky?

If this could be, if anyone here
were here with me inside the water and the wind
my home would flow through me and through anyone
and return to me, return to me in my sleep.

Humus

Without words or plans I was arriving
led by the surf, the days, the small streets and balconies,
worms and beetles came to fetch me,
by the waters of my homeless years I lay down gratefully,
ocean salts drifted in over my lips,
my eyelashes left like yachts on a further journey

I lay down, settling
so deep down, crumbling like bread
or the source of roses, honey, eggs

One by one my cells set out through tiny mouths,
atoms I knew moved along twigs, perched
on the tip of a thorn over some bird's wing feathers,
close enough to smell its arrival

Curiously my genes made proposals:
now the dune grass sings in a familiar voice,
a bed of succulents has grown pale and thoughtful,
the parapet of a building flicks its hair in the sun

All the while I lie here inside the seasons
watching the endless generosity of my bones,
mornings and planets keep coming to fetch me

Dispossessed words
found poem

*for Jessie Tamboer, who set herself alight and burned to death
because she could no longer provide food for her children*

Trucks carried 40 000 blacks to the southern edge of the desert.
I cannot say anything about my future now.
            We had a very beautiful view
            and this was the first time I saw my father cry.

They said 'Old man, are you moving?'
I took a crowbar, pulled the house down.
I cannot say anything about my future now.

★

            A man must have a dumping ground.
            Every rabbit has got a warren.
            A native must have a warren too.

★

Sometimes I cry, I
the absolute poor
I am sick to death of watching my ruin.

★

We had a very beautiful view of the sea –
            This was refused.

★

Uncovering rubbish bins, I ask, could it not be that something has been
     thrown in here –
just a little something that I can chew?

This was refused.

*

At times she would just suddenly start sobbing without any apparent
     reason.

The absence of love.
There is no way you can describe that hunger.
Shining clean pots and jars:
There was no food whatsoever in the house.

*

She was immediately engulfed by flames but did not utter a sound as she
     walked around the yard
burning.

The ashes of one household are collected by another for the bits of coal.
If you want to survive you must make a plan.

I cannot say anything about my future now.

The dialectics of love and uncles

All the way down there are conditions
to fall over the edge of, expeditions
of cells ferning in turns curving on
down over the edge and falling on
over the farther edge.

A serious bird pecks at the scruff of a winter palm
the day after its feathery intentions have unfolded, calmly
triangulating Darwin and Marx two billion years along God's graph.
Between mouthfuls, a claw intercepts some dust from a transitory planet's
        path
and whirls its way into a dragon's seed.
Nothing will ever be the same again in that family.

Necessary if not sufficient, this bifurcating hour
digs a road through history and a tower,
frothing in diamond drops over the edge of order.
Like a tiara unravelling, said the queen's warder.

And oh, my love, this crystal fire makes you more warm
than anything my breast has known these many centuries.
Stay with me as my words fly through the waterfall.
A breath to left or right could wake the dragon's need
uncurling in a fresh grain of time.

Now here its uncle is again, this memory of a dinosaur,
fat-voiced on a cold day, triumphant over the cousin on the sour-berried
        tree.
Stuck on the dispossessed tendril of the graph, all he can hope for
is a fractal kiss turning him like a key.

Still you continue unfurling your strange attractors,
the ones the ants around the sugar bowl obey,
curving up the edge of upwards –
and I the sugar in the ants' tears,
tumbling out along my own spiralling love
up over the upwards of your unmapped laughter.

Purposefully peeling footsteps

Words are such thin shavings of the fractal fruit,
tiny scrapings of the skin that holds
these joyously determined swirls of history
inside their juicy turbulence.

Talking itself westward after the day's feast,
each little word with its meaning strapped to its back
falls down the swell of tomorrow
like a hiker with hopeful new shoes.

The fossil's autobiography (abridged)

History's tank was mowing
down my resistance.
I was about to be

gone for good.
A smudge
embedded in a stone.

The stone that twitches
under each new plough
sowing freedom for strangers.

Anyone who'd walked
along the vector of my defeat
would have seen

me, leaping up, alive
going under and hopeful, insistently
eating the sunlight in the rising wheat.

All particles of my eradication
continue
flaring inside the hardening rock,
striking sparks off the future's dull blade,
not
quite
gone
yet.
Watch your step.

Jeremy Over

The poet writes to his family from New York

Well, here I am, alleluia, alleluia!
The sea voyage was marvellous:
six days of roses and cool hands.
What a sky I look for and am!

I am full of joy.
I live with drowned wasps and the legs of chauffeurs
in a drunk's lunch off Broadway, surrounded by canyons of lime,
where broken nightingales sing like bullfrogs in the Russian church.

My room is a capsule of air in saliva –
it is delightfully quiet.

Hippopotamus thighs and heron wrapped in rough canvas;
the meals here are a real challenge but I feel great.
I denounce everyone in feathers and plastic.

The American people are truly as naïve and charming as children –
they all carry candles and wooden spoons and this morning
they began to take a sudden interest in folding screens.
Needless to say I broke into tears.
This is the subject of my first poem.

But no one can imagine the loneliness an unstrung violin feels here,
especially when the priest lifts the mule.
No one except Mr Eliot, perhaps, who, shuddering with rage, in gold lamé
squeezes a lemon on the top floor.

Last night I went to 'The Laminated Cat',
The motley crowd of brightly-coloured sweaters,
tree trunks, clouds and turtles was resonant with
the delirium of astronomy and shepherd wrestling.

Next Sunday I plan to go to Coney Island
with some feeble-minded clergymen.
Like everything else here, it's a small,
small world with cloven feet in the pepper trees.

As you can see, I have begun to write in shoe stores
on stitched flesh at dawn. I lead a calm, quiet
sort of existence with white teeth in a box of twigs.
Such things are only sad from afar.

Yesterday I had a visit from little dead things dancing in the wind.
One of them made me a paper hat. I found it meaningless.

A pallid man asleep in a gardening glove is truly a child's dream
but when a thousand women sleep in a footprint in Peru
it is simply too much.

I may spend August in Canada.

And here's another strange thing – Walt Whitman,
with tiny red hands, bellowing at the roof's edge:
'LEAVE ME ALONE ALL OF YOU AND
I'LL LEAVE A PIECE OF CHEESE FOR YOUR DOG IN THE OFFICE'

Next time I write I will send you a copy of
The Slow Moustache (Cow Slobber) magazine,
which has published six photos of me covered with mushrooms –
I have a real following here.

I am going to Cuba for sure in March. Lorenzo has arranged the anthills.

Remember me to everyone
and tell Paco not to let the Pope dance too long on the dahlias.

Wrinkles, dreams, observations . . .

Ahead of his time, as usual, he smiled
on top of a hill, on a summer evening.
He was happy and the first to notice
that he was flying a kite.

Back at his house, on that horizon of emerald green ink,
the whole book of seaport colours lay open on his desk
beside slices of watermelon with a blue pitcher,
a sleeping gypsy, riverboats and pink paperflowers.

Later on, he liked to walk and talk barefoot on tamped earth
floors where too much bitterness would oblige us
to drink whiskey and get married.

'The truth is every sound,' he would always begin.
'I remember bells, the smell of cut lilies.
I remember an oblique stroking of the professor.
I remember you as a strange form of plaster monotony,
and, in another sense, I remember you, as a damp law clerk
howls inside a seashell, and breasts, yellow
as the yellow pigeon that is waiting on the far shore
are sauntering all around.

But now the hoarse are sleeping with wheat
in a big barn and I feel your purple face
would be marvellous in a coffeepot.

Oh spoonful of mud, I am looking at pieces of timber,
for every thick and mournful movement of bees
leaves a confused traveller and something
of the life of the lamp in the window,
chiselled, like breathing, out of mother-grief.

After so many years,
after so many dreams,
where is the panther I am speaking of?

I look at trees and see violets.
I have to sell kitchenware,
and I am sad.'

We applauded and raised our glasses as though he were still alive
with the kind of magic that finds, with growing astonishment,
a great eyelid in every stone;
an eagle amongst the rubble of the looting.

On other nights we probably looked at my uncles as much as his poetry;
nobody would have given them a thought otherwise.

Love Poem 5 a.m.

The last grains of the night
sift through the branches above our heads
as we step, on bare feet
through the young larches.

We are too much in love to eat
except for the occasional blackberry,
which we nibble at
like out of luck foxes
on their way home in the morning.

We are too much in love to sleep
but, for the first time that I can remember,
I have just had a vivid waking dream,
of weary swallows resting on the ground
in small hollows – pockmarks on the grass body
of a golf course by the sea –
scars in the turf left behind
by golfers after their shots
especially their approach shots
to the green where the steeply descending
chopping
motion
of
the club head
takes a rather

large divot
out of the ground
as backspin is imparted in order to stop the ball in as short a space
as possible.

This is sometimes tricky on seaside links, of course, where the often
sandy ground can drain quickly and become very firm, causing the ball
to travel a long way after the first bounce. In those sorts of conditions, I
always opt for the low chip and run approach myself: close the face of a
seven iron slightly and just sweep the ball off the turf like you were clip-
ping it off the dining room table. Better control and *no* divot.

That wouldn't leave anywhere for the swallows to rest though, I suppose –
No hollows for the swallows . . .

Absence
(After Neruda)

What's wrong with you, with us,
what's happening to us?
No! What's wrong with you, with you,
what's happening to you? I look at you
and I find nothing in you but two eyes,
two great dark eyes.

The rest of your body has disappeared.
Your knees, your breasts,
your waist,
are missing.

Your mouth and your lips
have just flown away.

Your hair and your skin
do not exist.

Why, why, why,
my love, why?

Where my love, *where?*
I ask you, where is your hair?

And your delicate hands – your slender feet
Ah! Your feet!

Take bread away from me, if you wish,
take air away, but
do not take from me your feet.

When I looked at the shape
of America on the map,
my love, it was your feet I saw.
When I could not remember who I was
I looked at your feet.

But you know that I love all of you,
your whole body,
those eyes of yours though –
I don't know – I do not dare,
I do not dare to write it,
those wild dark eyes,
those very big eyes were,
between you and me,
just a bit too big for your face.

Forgive me,
have I hurt you, my dear?
I do love your eyes, those sweet, most
capacious eyes.

There are rivers, there are countries
in your eyes,
my country is in your eyes.
I walk through them,
over hills,
next to the sea,
through villages,

across the road,
up the stairs,
walking, walking, walking.

Perhaps a day will come, small beloved,
when sleeping,
we shall walk through them together,
we shall walk all night long,
and at dawn
we shall see each other once more
face to face,
our love intact and new
and your feet,
refashioned,
together again.

Sinéad Morrissey

Before and After

I

'Agricultural high schools are the worst high schools in Japan.
The kids who swing through locked windows in Junior High
And masturbate in class come here, or ones not retarded

Severely enough to merit a house for the disabled,
All teeth and slurred speech none the less. They'll leave you notes
To tell you how they're injured in their heads.

A few are sons of farmers come to learn the trade,
But most have come with nowhere else to go.
The children who fall through the sieve of the system

Stop falling here for three years. Though if they rape
Or get arrested more than twice, they leave –
A free-fall to the bottom, the Yakuza or the sex trade –

We don't follow their sliding through. We're a thin membrane,
The box that holds the anger and the danger from the academic schools,
And the last cradle also. You can't *teach* here –

The children have no notion of oceans or algebra,
They'll want to know the English for sexual positions
And threaten you, perhaps, with aerosols and matches.'

II

I come back from school with baskets of persimmons, flowers
Sometimes, a bucket of miso, my head full of people vibrant and broken
Somewhere I can't see: all presents I hope I can carry.

At the Agricultural High School near Ogaki City, kindness falls over me
More than anywhere. Like the persimmons in your garden by Yoro Hill –
Enough colour in the mouth of winter to stop the cold.

Between Here and There

No one seems sure of the reason why aprons
Are tied to the necks of stone babies in temples.
The priest says 'honour'.
The guide to Kyoto City mentions 'cold
On their journey away from us to the heaven for children'.
I look at them squatting in Buddha-reflection,
Wrapped up to the throat in teddy bears and trains.

*

There's a graveyard for miscarriages under Ikeda Mountain
As stark as a bone-field. No flowers, tangerines, sake or aprons
But a basin of stone bodies in two parts: square body, round head.
Like oriental soldiers contained by a wall, they would go walking –
Spill over with all of the energy for life that fell out of them too soon.
Except that even in stone some bodies have opened:
Loose balls in the basin where heads have rolled.

*

Inside the biggest wooden building in the world
Sits Japan's greatest Buddha, one hand raised as a stop sign to evil.
The other is flat, flat with comfort and promise, flat enough
For all of us to nuzzle his thumb. His lily-flower opened.
His crossing was a falling into light.
Fall with me, he says, *and you'll be raised to the heights
Of the roof of the biggest wooden building in the world.*

*

When Nagasawa visits the house of the dead
He leaves at the door his camera and tripod
His champion karaoke voice his miracle foot massage
His classroom dynamics his rockhard atheism
And slips onto the tatami of the prayer room
As the man who can chant any you-name-it-soul
Between here and Ogaki to paradise.

Spring Festival

My body has become the body of the festival:
The vaginas on shrines reduce me to the facts of life.
And my wedding vows to you are this festival's promises –

A roaring in the ears, narrow entrances,
And the two of us hauled into life's own procession
Of mother after mother after mother.

Summer Festival

What do you think when you see a mâché vagina
Being rammed with a penis as broad as a battering ram
So that children disguised as elements shriek with joy?

You think: *we are disembodied, while the moon herself has a body.*
She is over by the beer-stands disguised as a man. One stagger and she'll trigger
The collapse of the dancers. The moon came to watch us and we all fell down.

Autumn Festival

The fields have been sealed with fire. They are singing
The promise of resurrection and revenge. The whole *cho*
Scraped of rice and fruit, it is time to go under and store.

On the streets I watch women who are dancing in rings
In the slow, hindered steps of the kimono. Again and again,
A festival of women. They are declaring what's been done.

Winter Festival

They'll padlock themselves with sake against the cold.
They'll bandage their loins. They'll straddle a drum on its side
Made from pulled skin and the sign of an upright swastika

And they'll move on a sea of bare men's shoulders, tall as trees,
Banging only when the silence has become unendurable.
In the alley there's a pyramid of bright flesh and lanterns, refusing to be born.

To Imagine an Alphabet

Too far back to imagine
It all was dissolved
Under soft black strokes
Of a Chinese brush
Diminishing the fatness
Of original things

Animal legs and human legs were emptied of flesh and blood

Patterns from flattened
Ants or a lake drained the facts
That are trees in Winter
The spokes of the world went down
In a language that
Went everywhere, stayed put

Put out what you want a woman and man to be the picture will hold
        that too

There are stories in skeletons
And after the three fluid
Lines that are Mountain, the four
That are Fire, Ice as a stroke
On the left side of Water —
Problem is Tree in a Box

I hear moaning and see constriction in a picture the colour is cinnamon
        the taste is chalk

A mind is inside the lines
All of it and sooner or later
Sex is everywhere, money
Rice-fields, wives are mostly
Under the roof, to Like
Is Woman with Child

I get lost in a landscape of noisy ideas that cross and flare in fireworks of
        strokes

Like a child who paints a smile
Over signatures makes Yin
And Yang (two kissing fish)
A rising sun in a field
Of wheat, I draw windows leaking
On the kanji for Rain

I make my moon round my forest has branches my people are walking
        with arms and a head

And then murder comes, a second
Killing, so softly I'm deaf
At the second of entrance.
My pictures defy the eyes.
I see Lamentation as five falling stars,
Grief abroad and walking,

And a terrible stag, flames shooting from his heart, as he prepares to walk
    and preach.

February

There is no kindness in me here. I ache to be kind, but the weather
Makes me worse. I burrow and sneer. I stay small, low, cheap, squander

All signs of the thaw by screwing my eyes. It's easier in the dark.
Defeat is the colour of morning, the grey that engenders the honeymoon
    flats

And the chess-board of rice-fields between this block and that.
Each field is marked

For the administering of cement, this month or the next.
I am living in boom, before the door-frames are in or the drive-ways
    drawn.

The new exit from the station to the South
Makes Nagoya spread, calls it out further than one city's insatiable mouth

Could dream. Factories chew through a mountain beyond my window
And each time I look at it it's less. In the world before the war

This place was famous: a stopping-house for the tired and sore.
There was one road only in Japan, and all who walked it walked through

This town. There are photographs of women in an amber light
Stopped dead in their surprise at being captured as the image of a time.

Behind them all, the mountain rises white.
They say it stayed so all Winter long, a shut door to the North.

The snow scatters now without it. When all the fields are town,
The mountain, stones, it will be Spring, and I'll be called on

To be generous. There will be days when fruit-trees, like veterans
Left standing here and there in pools of shade, will forget about use and
    bloom.

Lucidity

I

Every night he meets his family: is crumpled with his sisters
In a cellar, or watches as his niece becomes
Smaller and smaller until she disappears.

He hides boxes from his mother
That hold the bones of elephants, a warrant for arrest,
The shirts of her own buried father.

Caught either in scenarios of rescue, or with some
Bear-trap which he's used to trap and kill a man
In Mexico, he knows the man's his brother.

II

Awake, he never phones or writes
And seems so far away in life and mind
From where they are. Amnesia would be kinder –

Instead he wants to be a lucid dreamer, to enter
Whatever sea of fear and fever
Awaits him when he falls. He wants to change the colour

Of what's been seen and said, way back,
In the place
He can't remember or forget.

III

Suddenly he wanders, attaching
Notes to walls: *am I dreaming? If I meet*
My family, then I'm dreaming . . .

They cover the house and the whites of his daylight eyes.
Still, every night his family rises
And the smell of harm, the taste of damage

Invades him like the rush of a narcotic. He never knows he could escape it
With the thought: *this is a dream, and everything that happens*
Is a trick . . . until he wakes.

IV

There is an open sky, the kind you find
In desert in November. White clouds go over
At terrible speed. The sky

Is changing always. There are no ridges
On the land, no corners. At the end
Of everything, waving on the ledge

Of the world, pilots are stumbling to find
Their plane. And I am moving backwards, into the source of wind
While they grow

Smaller and smaller until they disappear.

Goldfish
for Joseph

The black fish under the bridge was so long I mistook it for
A goldfish in a Japanese garden, the kind the philosophers
Wanted about them so much gold under water to tell them what waited
In another element, like breathing water, they wanted to go
To the place where closing eyes is to see

I understood the day I closed my eyes in Gifu City I saw Japan
For the first time, saw what I had seen, the gate to the Nangu
Shrine by the Shinkansen stood straddled before my head and I
Held out my hands to touch it and felt changed air it wasn't
There but I walked into it continually and over the gardens full
Of pumpkin seeds in the ground and wild red flowers over them they
    told me

They brought Autumn and they were about my head also in Gifu City
    all pearled
In mist and happy as Japanese brides. I saw the JR crates on the night
Trains that passed through stations and seemed endless and running
On purpose on time's heels on sheer will to cross Honshu one end
To the other money's own messenger fire down the line. And when you
    talked me through

Gifu one end to the other eyes closed I saw what I would never
Have seen sighted a transvestite taxi driver set apart on the street
A lost person flowers by the pavement pavements for the blind I saw
Music as pulled elastic bands, drums as the footprints of exacting gods

I mistook the black fish for an oriental goldfish the flash of gold
On its belly meant it carried its message for the element below it
Always one storey down Zen masters attaining one storey down and I
Falling into you, story by story, coming to rest in the place where closing
    eyes is to see

Patrick McGuinness

Interior

Smiling, turning, faster than the shutter,
faces draw in the light, the bodies slide
into the deep room's furniture,
their outlines radiant, their white

unfinished lives still bristle up against
the surface of the world they left, which gives
them back, not at the moment when they stopped,
but at the moment, moving, when surprise

caught on the air around them and they span
into stillness in a trail of movement
which leads into as it bleeds out of them.

Not China but Tours

'I said I wouldn't fly again
For quite a bit. I did not know'
William Empson, 'Autumn on Nan-Yueh'

'If flight's as general as this'
Wrote Empson ('Autumn on Nan-Yueh'),
His England telescoping in,
His Europe dimming as he flew . . .
The landing gave flight's valences
Perspective, opened them to view,
So that his restless meditation
On what we fly from, flying to,

Sliced itself against both edges
   Of a single impulse, leaving two.
He walked on – his sands were shifting –
   Mine are sticking to my shoe.

'I have flown here, part of the way':
   My bed-desk-lamp triumvirate,
Four walls and window framing sky,
   Is the arena for the measured
Taking stock, the long-delayed
   Landing I hoped to profit by.
And in a sense it works, though my
   Flight (Air France), and my flight, postdate
Too much the things I fly away
   From, arriving here too late,
Wrong knots tied, right ones still to tie,
   And a familiar mess in wait.

Another Language

Writing was to build on paper;
To speak was to make things out of air,
To see was to take light, and shape it
Into something that was never there.

Solid Castles in the Air: Erik Satie on his Times

'People used to say to me: "Wait until you're fifty, then
you'll see." I am fifty. I haven't seen anything.'   Erik Satie

I

See how his supple, seated frame fills out
     its meticulous black suit
And how the sleeves begin, unseen, to sprout
     intricately into hands,
How they tenuously start to flout
     introversion's unilateral rules, expand
On loneliness in tonal sarabandes,

transfer crisp arabesques on air
     that like ivy curl
around the unseen columns
     of his solitude,
transcribe the patterned rows of birds
     on telegraph wires
or charm the backlit hieroglyphs from their
     cages into sound.

II (A Late Arrival)

They buried it, along with an anthology
Of its favourite possessions, and a few
Smells to give it ballast. 'Pince-nez', the
Sculpted beard, the ivory-tipped cane;
The absinthe fumes and smoke from cigarettes –
The age disappears behind particulars, the place
Dams up behind the welter of the details
It produced. A Paris locked inside its
Image, and I missed it, suitcases in hand,
As one misses trains, suitcases in hand:
Last songster for a decomposing time, this
Fleshing out between high-points of bone.
Now the gaps are all that matter,
My only matter. And Music? 'Free of Time',
They say, because it fabricates its own,
Makes up the rules it keeps to as it goes along.

Hard to be nostalgic, not having invested
in anything to remember; having only ever
lived the life to come, always, as a promise
to myself, ahead of myself. But no soul
is certain that it does not need to rise,
occasionally, 'symbolically', to elegise
an age that weaned it even in its passing by.
I join the dots until they too disappear: notes
that swivel on their axes and fold back into
pleats of air – their footholds, their occasions.

III

So still and resolutely *maudit*:
nothing, these limbs without a body,

this pose, tended so carefully to dispose
of itself between acts. Saint-Saëns

(*La République*) at regimental
ease, the orchestra at roll-call,

stiffened ranks of the *conservatoire*,
wooden batons churning empty air

like milk until it curdles in the bell-
dome of their medalled concert-hall.

Their carrots and their sticks, their small heroics
unclimb the scale in sleepy acrobatics.

Let me pitch the airy tent of *my* conservatory
            and down a disappearing path of sound
I'll make a void take place beneath a scaffolding of tune.

IV

The arms have tunnelled through the sleeves,
The sleeves have sprouted into hands,
The hands have parted into fingers and
        the fingers into keys.

The player folds into the jaws of his piano.

Birthday Poem
For Angharad Price

The window gives no clue.
Outside, the sun could be
another season's, but for the
cold you cannot see; the branching
cracks along the sky are tensed

to hold it up, things lock their edges
into light. This arbitrary day
you'll fill out with yourself, as through
the moving glass you see the trees
are rooted in clear air.

Heroes

I The Cowboy

> 'I think the sun, the moon
> and some of the stars are
> kept in their tracks
> by this Person's equilibrium'
>   Edward Dorn, *Gunslinger*

That 'some', *only* some, that measure in all
things, even when the praise outsoars the praised
but is never good enough, still falls
short though it takes in a world, entire skies

to give the airy Slinger ballast
and close his image in her words. Un-
bridled praise, but she holds back: no limits,
only frontiers for this superhuman

cowboy, slender in the sunlight of her eye.
Red suns burn to white. As she sees him leave,
saddling his talking horse, she thinks he'll fly
to join the things she can compare him with.

II The Celt

She watched the bright bird dying on the ground;
her lover climbed into the image she had made,
and there, until he came, he stayed.

The words were there ahead
of him. No beauty but was pulled, ready
from the world around.
She had not known him. When he came
it was himself he found.

I could love a man with hair black as a raven,
with skin like snow, whose mouth is the colour of blood

she said. He was already there. The same
dead white red black world he found
had shut him out inside another name.

The Darkroom

'The relatives could not recognise their dead from early photographs.'
H.B., photographer at the Paris Morgue, c.1890.

His first photograph was a building site in mid-
construction. Whether the *Rue Impériale* stands
ruined or in process, he cannot any longer tell.
The shutter had stayed open for a full half-hour,
drinking in the street it emptied; people
are invisible, who as they move make
no impression on the copper plate.
This, he thinks, is how ghosts are born.

★

He could be fishing for shapes, the room
could be a coastal shelf at night, quiet
in the aftermath of some catastrophe.
The sea could be a darkroom,
where black water licks its banks and waits.

Something lost, forgotten, puts on body
as he sifts among the wreckage. Rescuer,
alone, his hands are nets, drag back changed
forms of settled light, flat fossils, smoothness.

★

Not dead: asleep. The camera can euphemise
as much as language, as much as death
can put on shapes of sleeping, seem
temporary, hold its own reality at bay . . .

. . . thinking it would never be like this,
that his work was all creation, fixing living
people, things blazing in their worlds,
and his artless art uncovering the known,

finding as it found. They could not *see*,
amid these backlit vanishings, perfected
bodies, a resemblance: the world
was healing over them, growing back.

Oliver Marlow

There is a Path

There is a path goes right across a field,
High across the middle of a nothing sort of field,
A field of mostly grass.

I am here today,
Buffeted, hearing
Nothing but the blowing

Till I turn away,
And hear the quiet thunder of a distant aeroplane
Drifting into grey,

While all the time and all around
Busy songs of birds
Rise from the ground.

I can see behind
Two school towers,
Red, black, over green trees;

Ahead, a church's only tower,
Closer,
Nestled in by trees bringing out the grey;

Right, the downs going blue;
Left, a line of brown houses,
Sounds of building too.

Under me, mud gives to the push of a thumb,
Leaving an impression? Yes,
But not where I press,

On the thumb itself, the mud
Showing up contours of the skin,
The incline made by a pencil pressing in,

While all the time and all around
Busy songs of birds
Rise from the ground.

Someone Has Carved

Someone has carved a seat out of wood,
Where a copse has been cut back,
Almost like a kind of joke,
Someone showing that he could.

Come in close, you will see
How the shape of it is cut
Out of what
Remains of a tree.

Straight back, arm rests,
It almost is an armchair,
Backing on to where
A white sun sets.

Would you sit in it?
There's fungus,
And worse,
The seat will make you wet,

Give nothing in return.
I do,
Though
Not sitting down

Totally,
Finding it
A snug fit,
Tailor-made for me.

As a chill
Rises within,
I find I'm shown
Sunlight still

Touching tops of trees;
Higher,
Together,
All the sky's

Clouds going right
Over light blue;
Below,
A wall clean and white;

Above,
Under-wings of birds, a pair
Up in the air,
Trying to move.

I watch them battling,
Let the seat
Take my weight,
Hear a trilling

Like water spilling,
And what I see
Is a dead tree
Singing.

Here is Another Bridge

Here is another bridge:
Three trunks laid across,
Two large,
One
Smaller in between,
Laid across a stream
Of unreflecting ice.

Snow is in the air,
A flake,
One more,
Then
Nothing else,
As cold is on my fingers worse
When I stop my writing.

Engines from the sky and road
Are far enough to merge.
Constant, they never come distinct.
This bridge,
Whose cracks snow brings out,
With moss green smoothness,
And ice a final threat.

Lets you see between
Down where all is brown,
Except where leaves have lodged;
Has
Tied to a post the other side
Something mostly shiny green,
Perhaps to mark where someone died.

It's like a dead balloon,
And as my fingers lose their grip
I have to cross to see,
Step by step
Past the middle where it gives
And bounces up and back again,
Till I see the old balloon

Really is an old balloon,
Tied with care, like a sign
For a race perhaps.
Wedged,
I bring it back to life
Just by pushing part
To fill the other like a heart.

On the farther side, so what?
Brown growth and brambles,
Some fallen down trees,
A path,
Leading on and up
Past a pair of shoots
With a thousand prickles,

(But these have lost their power,
Their broken heads are bowed),
Up until a track-marked tractor track
Comes right across.
It brings me back to people; it is a proof of work.
Before, the lightest branch across my path,
One that I could easily

Snap between my fingers,
Makes me stop to see
Green becoming lighter brown
Near where it ends –
And there, catkins hanging down,
Two large, one smaller,
Tiny honeycombs.

I follow the branch back,
Past its own tributaries,
Back into the tree itself
Till I see
Trunks, a cluster coming up and out
Bringing me to see
Three's everywhere, against a light sky.

A Mile from Gibbon Mill

Where barbed wire lies on nettles to the left,
And brambles warn out from the right,
You come to a seven bar rust brown gate
Just off the road and out of sight.

An insect goes across the top,
Rust both ends, crocodile low,
A little bit of tropics
For this part of Sussex.

Branches overhang the gate.
Between, there is a view of a field
Down to rust coloured trees,
And then beyond to further fields,

Trees, an occasional rust coloured roof.
There's nothing in the field – thistles, holes,
No life except what looks like a llama lying down,
And is a llama lying down,

Head up, like a Loch Ness monster,
A little bit of elsewhere.
Head down, it could be a log,
Just as the pads of a tropical frog

Are really the buds of a nearby bush,
The flowers, the stars of an African night,
The leaves, an elephant's wrinkled skin,
The bar I am stroking left to right

The hide of an old rhinoceros,
Chained both ends, never quite tamed,
With flies around or on its back, and bits of fur
Further down, where the skin is rougher.

Above, a pulse of birds is in the trees,
As my special fly
Opens its wings
And is caught against a grey sky

Before turning into trees,
Part of a wood
Going back from the fence,
Rainforest dense.

Patrick Mackie

Faces with Dusk and Rain

When I stepped gently into the road, suddenly
it was raining. As well as raining,

it was dark, the dusk plump with clouds.
My face was still full of her kisses on my cheek

when I saw the motorbike I was face to face with:
it almost wiped her smile right off my face.

★

And then, on top of everything, her face broke
into laughter, her eyes merrily screwing up, her smile
creasing itself. Her hair became a mess of wet

happiness, getting shaken and rained on. The rainy
dark was lacquering everything, plunging. I gawped
when I saw what fun the dark and rain and shaking

were making of her hair, how her face was a place
for her hair to be all over. I noticed how each hair
was as streaming and as moved as the dark rain.

★

Glad to be alive, not walking but sauntering,
looking both ways along each dusky street,

I smiled on everything
being rained on, exultant that

my face and hers would alike be alive with rain.
I felt ravished by each gently plump drop.

What We Have Seen

The beauty of a woman or of wise hearts, or of gentle knights
in armour; the song of birds, or a conversation about love;
bright-coloured ships moving quickly on the sea; the clear air
when dawn appears, or white snow falling without any wind;

the water in a stream, or a meadow filled with every kind of
flower; gold, silver, or the azure used in ornaments – these are
beauties, you'll agree. Yet we have seen what we have seen,
there was no looking away from it, no weeping it away,

and it is not yet time to begin again. We haven't the energy.
We've been sleeping badly recently – you know how moths
can take to blundering inanely around a bedroom for hours –
and the moon insists on changing just a little every night

to keep us on the look-out. So we remind ourselves of the comforts
no one usually thinks to mention, the pleasures of stretching all
round the bed in stages, the joys of the different levels of darkness,
the reinvention of beauty as a pet name for insomnia.

That Was Then, This Is Now

Isn't it just unhappiness? Everything's different
from how you conceive it, the grass still flutters easily
in the breeze, there are still bees faffing around in the many-
hued flowers. All that will continue, like any landscape, as far

as the eye can see. But there's a mood, like a gust taking
a page by surprise, bringing vestiges of something else, remnants,
mere flickers of what you wore. To talk of the Hitchcock films
you'd both seen, or even just to mention that bar's gaudiness,

with its combination of neon lights and Mexican
paraphernalia, would be something – the rural scene, well,
blushes at the thought. Of course, the radiant flatness
with which sunlight normally slaps itself down like paint

will prevail, a certain sheen settles things for you, and such images,
even what little bits of them there are, can only float
inappropriately like a colourful insect in cola, no more vexing
than being kept awake by listening to someone fall asleep.

Up

This image is of an outdoors swimming pool suddenly rising
clear into the air on a hot afternoon, keeping its shape
while the swimmers in it keep swimming, seemingly
not noticing as it levitates out of the ground and gradually

up

to about the level of the taller trees, where it hovers
in the sunlight, and the three or four swimmers in it splash
around, making waves that slap and quiver against the air.
Then the pool descends back down into the concrete.

The Unnecessary Angel

As evening came, a man was seen wandering out into the fields. The hills
trembled with calmness. Birds were flying in swift formation swoops. His
presence was felt in the strained-into, somehow bright dusk.

★

Having come here to hear rain slurped quietly by the springy spring ground, having come to feel the soaked grass give surprisingly lushly underfoot, to see the rich layering of forms around the edges of the woody areas, to notice the distant swishing of streams, the thrushes singing then not singing, or the infinitesimal darkening of the rough hill-tops, to watch the dim shadows of flying birds touching the twitching branches, to try to see air, he walked and walked.

*

So the condition became one of enormous width. This of course is indescribable, but think of it as a kind of failure of anything to be near anything any more: the surroundings expanded, the expandings surrounded: at every juncture distance loomed, at every cross-roads the two roads turned out to have another hundred yards before they met each other, leaves dangled far off from their branches, fluttering against the dull sky, and the branches were in any case suspended in the air, far away from their trunks, while the birds spread from each other into isolated corners of the panorama. He came to feel a certain sensation of flotation, a basic airiness. When he spoke, his voice raced ahead of him to the horizon, pronouncing in every direction things he had not yet thought of.

An Emotion Constitutes a Magical Transformation of the World

A deepening ensues – like the feeling of watching
the chiaroscuro being added to a charcoal portrait of yourself

after you've finished posing. You can do nothing now but witness
the accretion of shades – the plush layering – a revelation by smudging.

A Translation (i.m. Octavio Paz)

As through a magnifying glass, the light lights – quickly becoming flame.

Gone – gone – where? – To what region of being? – To what existence
in what worlds?

Like the kingfisher seen as a flash of topaz, the twigs weave as flame.

It opposes. My hands uncover. All the suns now become. I write.

Window in immensity. There is no one here. Presence without name.

Last night an ash-tree, right on the point of declaring something, didn't.

So that the disappearance of matter into light – magnificence –

Apparition. Golden Lotuses. Distant Neighbour. Exclamation.

A house, a garden spin, come and go. Each caress lasts a century.

The remains of sparks. The jacaranda's fireworks. A sun each day.

From colour to form – the tip of each flame both fire and air – from
form to –

I write without knowing the outcome of what I write – it shines elsewhere.

You are beside me. Your thoughts are black and golden. To extend a
hand –

And time's wound be an invisible scar, scarcely a delicate line.

And the poem be one single interwoven word, a strong radiance.

So that if space is a place of impalpable nuptials, this marries.

In place of a loss – the sun reflected in fire reaching into air.

The Manifestations

It's your face seen in a curved mirror.
It's two faint green spotlights in the night-sky.
It's what you know you won't know when you see it.

It's the invisible turbulence of air-waves.
It's the sumptuous billowing of some trees.
It's not exactly something you get used to.

It's the thought of crowds endlessly milling there.
It sounds like a whole orchestra improvising.
It's the weariness of forever seeking it.

It keeps taking your eyes off the road.
It's a plastic bag floating to the sky.
It has the evanescent darkness of cigar smoke.

It's the arbitrariness of changing moods.
It is suddenly hidden by your shadow.
It's also the moistening dew and the sky a-quiver with song.

It looks right through you like a portrait.
It's in the shy blue flame of an oil lamp.
It's difficult.

It's a sudden huddled noise, like a threat.
It's not knowing which buttons to press.
It knows which buttons to press, however.

It's the heart beating with surprising ferocity.
It looks like pleasure, but it feels like pain.
It's wrapped within a stone within a dove within a bear.

It's in the swollen yellowness of some summers.
It's an unearthly tune on the harmonica.
It's the life that you do not lead.

The End of Something

These places don't need us, and the conversations we've been holding
about love can no longer be justified solely by the physical charms
of the people seated around us, however shinily lissome,
not now that their ramifications are becoming clearer and

clearer. It isn't just the fact that, somewhere not too distant, storms
will probably be impressively breaking, booming around and casting
sudden light on the faces of casual passers-by – though who are we
to turn that down? – nor is it merely the thought of the unceasing

glow of sunset we might live in if we worked out how to circle the globe
at exactly the right speed to keep pace with it, that is shaking things
up. No, it would soon have been time anyway for us to abandon
these oak-panelled interiors, jettisoning the ingenious cigarette lighters

and the fake manorial portraits, and move on to speaking more freely
in front of more indefinite backdrops. We will take the lift and enjoy
making faces in its darkish mirrors, until somehow even descending feels
    like
being released from gravity, passing through clouds into thinner and
    thinner air.

Emma Lew

Riot Eve

I haven't, thank God, become a perpetrator.
I never caused the death of others, though I must utter these words.
I hold myself back, as the shrewd son of my father.
I see it like this: a lion will attack a gazelle.

We have one life. Why spend it being feebly decent?
We see but one night; we contain others.
I ask myself if this path and all those terrible detours were really necessary.
There is a reason for everything, and our catastrophe.

Imagine then that a father returns and doesn't speak about any of this.
He carries me on his shoulders during the long walk in the forest.
Imagine a man so polite, so clean;
his swiftness, his warmth, his murderous ideas.

Look, nothing in this world is perfect.
This is the condition, now growing darker.
History has shown us: the Inquisition, the Black Death . . .
I await the real wooden anger that shapes me.

The gardens have roared for days.
The wind bends the trees. It is like a sign.
I hear of a palace rising.
It is just after midnight, and I will obey you.

Fine White Hand

You came to my room, you moved books.
I accepted things from spirits.
A trance gathered in my house.
Who were you when you were on earth?

The horse plunges, and I wake.
The bed shakes, and I know it is you.
So many knocks, so many knocks.
An egg leaps down to crack itself.

I call you *light*, for the room is pierced,
and my head has a wind in it.
I see you in your light fire dress,
three feet from the floor and beckoning.

Past-midnight is never-ending.
What are you that troubles me?
You seem to be only half in this world.
I can promise nothing to ghosts.

Is it my mind that travels at night
to places that we do not know?
I have seen life madly beautiful.
I am, and now I'm nothing any more.

If the table moves, let the pressure be so gentle.
Smash the glass and give me air.
I wander in the garden with no bandage on my eyes.
I'm compelled by strange force to cry with you.

Sinking Song

You, me, money and fear –
the rings of planets through our hands.
We are just strong enough
to make the tides work for us.
We could move in the veins of orchids.

In the wonderful phrasing of this evening,
fire runs along us as a man.
All vanished animals weep,
and cities, built merely to fall,
drown in birds.

Come, trust the world –
it's still night,
and the moon wishes to dissipate,
and earth groans under its weight of mice,
and God has given us everything, everything.

Poem

Decaying thunder,
all the ordinary rain.
A raft of tiny fools,
a poem of nails.

Pursuit

I have not had fortune but I have seen the resplendent moths
of Daghestan. I have travelled through clusters of their castles
and found them wingless, lain deep, like the oak apple.
And in Angola I have seen hundreds of butterflies grieving.
I have seen butterflies swerve like the fiddle and the bow.
I once heard a boy sing on the deck of a Black Sea steamer:

There is a small and fragile bug!

                                        The respiration,
the pulses of the heart, the beating that bursts the lid
of the shell. In sago I found the weevil itself, and I smelled
the perfumes of the males. Often I've dreamt of the wasp's
tumbled journey, the mosquito's guilt and thrift, how the ant
slipped down to haunt the grass, how the hornet left only
the skin of my fruit. For insects have a beauty that hurts,
and that may even darken the sky. They drum with
their bellies upon the twig. They have learned to cleanse
their blood with light. I have seen a mantis of a delicate
mauve impaled on the flea's single spine. I have known
the mere segmented grub, and I have shared the earth with
lice. In the forests of the Congo, I recorded the stickiness
of swarms. O unforgettable flies of Palestine! O cicadas
of Spain in the year I was born!

The Tale of Dark Louise

Must there always be some stray hungry suitor?
I strive and I struggle, I can't keep the wolf
On the day foretold by the travelling scholar
I take my hank of flax and ride out
The herring in the sea fall into a trance
I put on the dress that brought me this shame

Fire is never out of my chamber
And the convent's interdiction falls between
I'm not beautiful, but my eyes are drunk with music
I will write whatever I want on your soul
The vine is heavy again with the sweetest grapes
And the ale flows, and the cellar drowns

Berchtesgaden

She tells a strange story of Hitler's love of astrology
She saw Goebbels with a red weal on his face
She says Hess is an addict of heroin
And says of Himmler *He still suffers from the effects of*
venereal disease contracted when he was only
a lad of twenty
Coarse Goering is always cracking jokes
Contrary to popular belief, the Führer is a late riser
Lunch is his favourite meal and begins with vegetable soup
He has a passion for trout served with butter sauce
Sweet potatoes usually accompany the fish
Sometimes an eagle is seen circling in the blue air
Guests assemble on the balcony before the dinner hour
Munich radio brings them *Die Lustige Wittwe*
Rounded forms of crockery gleam in the great hall
The Führer's pockets are always filled with chocolates

Chernobyl: Small Talk

I feel that I can trust you with a secret:
I've been ordered to fall in love with you
and I'm insanely worried about my eyes.
To this, add the collapse of my own
private world. I would kiss you
but am afraid to soil myself.

I'm inaudible. I'm babbling and my hands
are in a constant state of motion, for
love is immortal and lingers on
in dreams and waking visions. A fanatic
is not expected, but allow me to hanker.
Come over, the apples are ripe
in my guardian's orchards.

Something about the way you dance
reminds me that I have to sit down.
We are beautiful as long as we are masked,
and treachery is an affectionate game.
Like a circus, I cover my heartache.
Soon my mistakes will make me famous.

They Flew Me in on the Concorde from Paris

They flew me in on the Concorde from Paris.
We were fortunate not to burn.
Over Shanghai I observed to my flautist husband,
'Such a metropolis needs a decent opera house.'
He rejected me in late May.
I resolved in future to express my feelings through my garden,
With an archway of zucchinis and cucumbers,
A bed of apothecary roses and high-yield grass seeds.

In the carpark at the Institute of Space Research
Women workers were performing their role of holding up half the sky,
While shipping companies complained about reserves of grain
Silting up the anchorage and all the sputnik could do was bleep.

I lodged with a senior government official in four elegant pavilions
Named after four seasons and bedecked with imitation sheep carcasses.
It was almost unthinkable not to give,
But I had no hard currency and could not afford contraceptives.
Thus I took a tonic in winter to be able to hunt tiger in spring.

I delivered my acceptance speech in the Great Hall of the People.
Citing the Scripture of Mountains and Seas,
I began by calling on steel makers to take up the way of Lamaism.
'Let's start calming down!' I cried.
'Let's get off painting and onto banking.
Differences are secondary to common interests,
They should not affect bilateral ties in a larger sense.'

I was applauded by reformists and conservatives alike.
Tell that to the lady in the morgue.
And tell her,
'When you get to heaven,
Maybe you'll get some answers.'

Thebes

I think of you as you are
at noon. One cloud in
a clear sky, oh that
one cloud! Your days
are like smoke, wild
as prophets. Fruit fallen,
throats to the dagger.

A dead language in
the blood. A fury locked
in the body crepuscular.
Ghost town, torn and
white. All I ask you
to do is radiate.

Stormlight and the
coming-on of night.
Moan of planets, mice
on the path. The dark
charge of doors and
the lake that burns.
Every method of howl
shaping the swoon.

Nicole Krauss

The Last Eunuch
On the fall of the Manchu Dynasty

In those final years,
scribes and tailors dismissed,
a gold nightingale
nesting under the bed,
I dreamt of a man
weeping over an onion.
A wick in peanut oil
cast more shadows
than kerosene
and behind a paper screen
a wild mango rushed
like a barbarian.
And after the white rain
a green swell rose
in the garden,
or the moon appeared
like a watermark:
tyranny can't grasp
all things, and what
slips from the palm
leads elsewhere, like footprints
in spilt flour, or a rickshaw
through the lime trees.
Since then
I have befriended
the barbarians.
Who else could fathom
the width of an empire,
six hundred leagues of wall
and through a chink,
the future.

New World

for Matthew Johnson

Anduve como vosotros escarbando
la estrella interminable
y en mi red, en la noche, me desperté desnudo,
única presa, pez encerrado en el viento.
                                        – *Neruda*

Il cammino fisce a queste prode
che rode la marea col moto altero.
Il tuo cuore vicio che non m'ode
salpa già forse per l'eterno.
                                        – *Montale*

You, the good student of islands,
              must live by now
on the other side of the wind's wall
              where a parrot
wings and disturbs nothing
              as nothing is more
              or less than itself.

Under the pavilion of stars,
              no captain's gramophone
plays a ballroom tune, and a New World
              slips from the map
and the storyteller begins to feel
              a thousand-and-one tales
              is not enough to live.

Here, things are still what they seem,
              and if you dream
at night don't feel guilty. From
              where you stand
the world appears flat, and perhaps
              it is; perhaps
              the eternal return

will also be trapped like a fish
    held up in the wind.
As it stands now, you've no defence
    against the horizon,
such a precise argument against
    lasting happiness.

So in these bleached Pacific years
    accelerate toward
not knowing exactly, and at night
    beneath the dome
of your skull, when you stare up
    at the low-slung cosmos,
    keep in mind that I,

too, have wandered against what
    others hoped for me,
not for exploration's sake but my own
    sense of motion,
where wings pressed to the chest can cure
    a fever and every island
    creaks at its moorings.

Bartolomeu Dias Remembers the Flat World

Note: that in December of this year 1488 Bartholomaeus Didaeus comman-
dant of three caravels which the King of Portugal had sent out to Guinea to
seek out the land, landed in Lisbon. He reported that he had reached a
promontory which he called Cabo de Boa Esporança . . . He had described
his voyage and plotted it league by league on a marine chart in order to place
it under the eyes of the said King. I was present in all this.
             – *Christopher Columbus*
             (in the margin of folio 13 of his copy of Imago Mundi)

It's true: after a while one grows tired of salted fish,
of reading the same books, of the on-and-on of space.
The eye plays tricks and you let it: there's little use
for porpoise tails, but of mermaids the need is endless.

All my life I feared reaching the end of that gaze,
that a common cloud would lift and I would find my ship
parked on the silver ledge of horizon, and me face to face
with imagination. At times I believed vision would slip

or end there, for surely the eye depends on some limit,
some terse frontier to put the view into perspective.
Or maybe not. Maybe having arrived at the end of the line
which has stubbornly rhymed sea with sky, the eye would give-

in to a whole new verse, and as the foot lost its grip
on terra firma, a flock of angels would sift into focus.
But these are lofty thoughts for a sailor. One tries
to do his job, keep the latest tyrant happy. Of course

if Pero d'Alenquer hadn't been such a lech, waxed his moustache,
hedged his bets, and boasted to the court that his scarlet
stockings were from India, I might not have found myself
coasting toward the Congo with that buffoon for a pilot,

and nothing but a rain-soaked map and an astrolabe
with which to find the route east. Let no one
tell you differently – history is fuelled by vanity.
But you know the rest. Except maybe this: the reason

I called that cape *Tormentoso* was not just because a storm
had pulled us into its grainy hem and skimmed
us round the horn to safety, but because when it cleared again
some wild, unchartered corner of our view had been broken-in,

and beyond those headlands one world ended.
When we returned to Portugal with nothing but that name –
which would later be changed, too – a lanky, ambitious *inconnu*
was present in the stalls, a nobody who would one day win fame

for wrapping the world round its axis. The future, I'm sure,
will worship him. As for me, I often wonder why we didn't
buy wholesale into time; for there's only so much space
a person can use, but of time the need is infinite.

New Science

1

The blind fingers of another thought
brush you: light in the oak trees,
the sound of great distances. How long
the road is between here and uncertain clarity,
the fossil of each idea you have worked
into wood. If you make space in the morning
perhaps it will come to you, an arrival
of wings across the roof. So many months
have stalled you in this place so that now
the windows frame your own face
looking back in at who left long ago.

2

Beneath the oak is buried another
story, rain-soaked and wild-eyed,
turned green and vanished. The trade of kites
in a darkened wind reminds you of pilots
who broke-in the sky so that now only the stars
and the future are mysterious. Sewn into Pascal's coat
was the answer to all this, simple as his circle
which holds you now. Long after everything
is given up for lost a part of speech returns to you
and a new science measures its weight
not in an apple but the fall of acorns.

3

In winter you enter light to change yourself,
glass cracking in the trees where the sun ignites
a hollow afternoon; how well you understand
this dissolution. One day the idea will come
for the Arctic, a mathematics so perfect
it retires into imagination, and you will tell its story,
especially you, knowing of what metal the future is made.
Because even when the diamond sellers let loose
their dogs, and the enlightenment bursts out
in the trees, in the shadow of the lamplighter's cape
a new Quasimodo must hurry past, and only you can hum his tune.

4

Much later, after the clatter and smoke
had cleared, you looked round and saw
that an age had ended, at a moment unaware
of its own importance, perhaps it began to rain,
the smallest, most insistent change, now lost
in the annals of North. After all these years
the wolf is still dressed in sheep's clothing,
the time is still your own, and you realise –
between the things you had to say and the things
you could – there may be another way, a getting back
to the first person, the one who started all this so long ago.

Quarters

1

In winter, in morning, north seems more thing
than idea. It slips in bed with you
directing your last dreams towards waking.

Things take on a Scandinavian odour,
and the older your lodgings are, the colder
your feet will be. Between a lover's ear and shoulder

is the snuggest place you can think of.
Space turns white instead of a shadowy grey,
and your pallor lightens by instinct, so as not to betray

your face. There is a need to go unrecognised
in winter, to follow the same route both ways.
Seeing someone you know, try to look away.

2

The bastard spring comes early, disowned by March.
There is something vaguely offensive about tulips,
so stupidly pleased in the face of what is serious.

May gives the landscape a competitive flavour,
so all beasts and plants try to outdo their neighbour –
an excess of petals, plumage and sling-back heels.

Meanwhile the day feels the need to allongé,
stretching out its stay and forcing you
to do sexy things while it's still light out.

Now that your hands have left your pockets,
you use them for punctuation. They often wander
from their own situation, taking liberties until told to stop it.

3

Heat, unlike cold, is tolerant of the aromatic,
and summer stinks of itself: everything hectically
blooms are turns rotten while the season stays simple.

There is something faintly static about summer,
the way friends linger over a cold tumbler,
the way speech shirks its winter responsibility to purpose.

Suppose time weren't so regular, it might bend
lazily around summer, as if taking the long way.
Things get lost in August: columbine, delphinium.

4

There is always a coming-back-to, a noticeable shifting
towards beginning again. The long spell of nostalgia lifts,
and shapes disguise themselves less. Air is more like water,

warm pockets alternating with cool. Autumn brings clarity,
the way the cold and light cut and contain everything.
This is the season where you least need company,

not cold enough to want their heat, nor bored enough
for their distraction. The day is less curvy and tangled,
moving austerely, in scarce right angles.

How odd, the way we never waver from this round trip.
Could there not be some slight, overlooked path
leading off towards an ill-defined, intemperate arrival?

Stephen Burt

Letter from Minorca
after Jaime Gil de Biedma

After the distant nightclubs and their piers
had cut off lamps for curfew, quiet laws
descended on our island
and on our neighbours inland;
a fingernail, a residue of light
rose up before dawn on the facing beach –

a thoughtful phosphorence, a thin gaze,
a parachute afloat. So near that sea,
from the planning-mistake of the wooden boulevard,
where we waited for hours for the townies' night
to shut down for us, there seemed to fly toward us,

again and again, the sense of being enormous,
part of the atmosphere, clarified, so that the docks,
their rush and scrappy nettles, took up space
nowhere, or just *inside* the two of us . . .

Next day was your last there. All the flat sand
gathered and lapsed in bodies of its own,
bodies that lay on one shoulder each, and could cry,
for love, all day in stiff clouds without tears.
If you kissed them they tasted of oysters and nectarines;
from far away, they smelled like liberty.
When you fell asleep outdoors, late and alone, nostalgia
grew like a bloom over envy and desire,
nostalgia for what you must have considered another
age of the body, of unrefined desire –

Not desire alone; also the sense
that someone desired you too. It is this dream,
the same monotonous dream through adolescence,
the same old dream, of course, and more remote
each time it happens. Shame, erosion, prudence –
wrecking and excavating old foundations
to put up new resorts – collect from love,
as from old dune-walls, all the stones it has,
dismantling it for wisdom or for money . . .

Tomorrow, no moon in the daytime; no sea; the City,
pink angled marble, beams, a kind of beauty;
standees on trains, a kind of library.
The night after tomorrow you will sit up,
still sleeping, and remember the sand on the bodies:
El Dorado, the given,
the gold, the choosy, the brazen
untainted because unattained, the ones you will never
know if you could have known; and the imprecise grace
of knowing that, at least, will get to you
like a slap in the face; you will swivel, smart, and see
nobody has touched you – what do you owe, anyway,
and to whom? – and wake up half-erect
already, and have forgotten even that debt.

The Alders

after Jaime Gil de Biedma: Ribera de los Alisos

which by corrupt or accustomed speaking they commonly call the
Elder . . . doth serve . . . to lay the foundations of buildings upon,
which are laid in the rivers, fens, or other standing waters, because it
never rotteth in the water, but lasteth as it were forever.

(OED)

The banks are much too old.
                              The path goes down,
dirty from sand and full of scratches, bruised
like all the scratches I wore as a boy;
abraded rootlets stick out here and there.
Telescoped, down the river, the knotted poplars
seal everything off – are all I can want from the world,
from this world, as its gestures show me back
into the first few seasons of my life.

A tiny corner of the map of Spain
is what I know of memory, was my one kingdom;
fixed, sheltered, here, I imagine myself there,
no time has passed –
I am six, that age
at which one goes to bed certain to sleep,
and wakes, with eyes defiantly still closed,
laid out along the bed on winter mornings,
and imagines a favourite day, the previous spring,
suffused by plain and calming odours,

pines? But these things change – are hard to notice;
abscond into leafmeal, or into the path itself,
the path I have been undoing by walking it.
Such sleeps, such grade-school dreams, are indices,
and all I remember of them are images:
one night a horse, one night the birth,
terribly impure and difficult, of the moon,
or the high flashes of a river approaching
carrying under it many years, floods in September,
the exaltation and fear of being alone
when I was walking late to school and knew it –

before these thoughts, there are no others;
I would know what I was if I knew what I could have called them.
And I know there is nothing we see that does not mix up
beauty and truth; still,
the beautiful hieroglyphs, images poured from a story,
are not the whole story –

there were, too, so many months of October,
of coming home after dark singing, when the wind
of autumn put its knife blade to my lips,
and of excitement in the family room
twinned with the fire, when nothing was unfamiliar:
the rhythm of the house and of wooden train stations,
the sweetness of an artificial order,
rustic and thinly spread, like a mat of peat,
a life like one of the woodsmen or grenadiers
who stood, steamed flat forever, on my wallpaper.

How can I simply stand above it now
or simply resent what I must have wanted then?
But how can I not see there the books of accounts,
the comical ghosts of school-fees, no slight wind
or specialised valley has yet been able to calm?

                    The farther boughs
like brushes play their snare drums in the wind,
and something else gets ready to grow dark,
as jumbled as these alder needles, as far
below me now as the vertiginous stream –
a softening, profound affinity
for nature where there is none, for company
wherever I think there might be none to be found,
and a fear of what is, before which these points and blades,
each pointing its unsheathed way to the one far creek,
seem far from me again; I am far from myself,
and the sash of the water, the banks with their needles, their alders,
are flimsy, antique, too sad to disregard.

After the Death of Jaime Gil de Biedma

after Jaime Gil de Biedma

Across the patio or in the garden, reading,
the house's shadow obscures
the page; the penitent cold, the end of August,
turns my thoughts backwards, to you.

This garden and its house approach
the birdsong in the complicated trees;
the absence of August, when it grows dark, gets lost,
and your book falls from my hand like the end of the year

in which you died. If only, in that winter
of your last sights, you have been given a glimpse
of sweetness, a taste of light! But I don't

think so. What I want to remember now
are not the hours, the last year,
of your beating your head against cabinets, drunken months, bruises
you collected, old coins, lining your body
like a too-tight clown suit . . . the others come back,
the year before and the year before and the years
before those years, and wash away
the only time we couldn't photograph.

It's your garden. It's August. Wine in vases,
tipsy incursions into your swimming pool,
soft heat under the trees. Voices bring
names: Angél, Juan, Marcelino, Maria
Rosa, Joaquina – Joaquina first of all,
the girl with the whispery, almost-invisible breasts.
The telephone laughed and you came back outdoors
and more of us, you said, would be on their way.
I remember, then, your one-yard run,
the flash of your body exploding into the water.

And nights of total liberty
in your enormous house: everything was for us,
as if we had occupied an abandoned convent,
destroying nostalgias, pulling up secret doors,

sprinting here and there through the open bedrooms
prying open the closets, alternately
amusing ourselves standing naked and fancily-dressed,
dusting off, for ourselves
to wear, short gowns,
high boots and slacks, making arbitrary scenes,
the old erotic dreams of your adolescence,
or of everyone's, of a boy left by himself.

Remember Carmina,
Carmina who came late, plump, tiptoeing downstairs
showing us her backside, wobbling
because she held up, in her left hand, a lit candelabra?

Then there were the corresponding months
and months of pain, of paralytic mornings,
the last night of pills and vomit over the carpet.
Later I saved myself, at least, by writing
'After the Death of Jaime Gil de Biedma'.

Between us, you were clearly the better writer.
Now I should know what the point of it was, your desire
to dream only ironies, of the muffled romances
in your poems I like best – for example, in 'Pandemic'.
How can I know what my poems would have been without you?

But sometimes I think it was me, in the end, who taught you.
– Who taught you to take over my old dreams
out of my cowardice: who ruined your own.

Christ in the House of Martha and Mary, by Velázquez

Because her home is someone else's castle,
She stands in our end of the picture, braced
Against her wet wood table and brass pestle
    Where shadows splash diffuse
Stormclouds across the bone-dry masonry.
Dismembered cloves of garlic that refuse
    To grind themselves to paste

Tally before her like a daisy-clock
The hours she has stood for, supervised
    By an arthritic, pocked,
Sad woman mentioned nowhere in the Gospels –
The hours which four perch, slim silver bells,
    Have spent shinily pending
Dismemberment to feed a house of five

And God Himself spent lecturing to Mary.
Seen only through a draughty, shade-chilled square
    Hole cut into a wall,
Christ, Lazarus and Mary rest, secure
Sun, Mars and Venus of an orrery,
Resplendent in their sense of an unending,
    Simple and categorical

Exemption from all earthly labour, granted,
    However, only to the first
Dozen or so who have the luck to take
Advantage of His offer. For the rest –
    Sceptics, the housebound, day-to-day
Providers, younger sisters and the like –
The kitchen table and a sullen duty.

    – So Martha thinks,
Looks bitterly to us in ruddy silence
Only because she has no one to thank.
    She wants to be rescued;
Her full lips pursed, she looks about to cry
And won't do. We're her only audience,
Or else Velázquez is, who, not yet twenty,

                    Abandoned his Seville's
Provincial tutors and unleavened houses
To strut his brushwork for the court and King,
            And brought Madrid this canvas
Recording the albedo of two eggs,
The weft of hair, the gamut of fish scales,
And the half-stifled hopes of all the young

Who, while the bright elect practise, converse
            And hope to be immortal,
Grind garlic, skin the fish and set the table;
            Who, were the tables turned,
Might say their faith in art or faith or manners
Counts more than the dull skills they never learned,
Then sit down calmly and expect their dinner.

Arriving Clouds

To notice dispassionately the blotchy, squared-
Off glass frontier of the International School
Across the walk is to know
Their world was too large: its allies keeping
Still, the ginger children who have fled
Out over railings, through each recessed door,
Will come back soon; I'd like to call them ours,

If they haven't been claimed. Then a white
Lynx crossed my path. Tolerance and
Withdrawal are valid models (she said) of all things,
From space travel to nutmeg and to love:
You get what you want, need more, and with extraordinary
Timing and cuisine they need you back.
Their names are Princess, Vitamin, and Reliable.
They run up great phone bills. To tell

The truth, I'm practically next to Texas
Here: the scarp of the south tip,
Its large flat handle, and then the uneven slides
That wouldn't touch given all day. It comes with peppers,
Raucous, auricular, rice- or sugar-
Filled, and small; around them we bake dust
In frosty shapes cut out to look like doves
Or hamburgers, or like the conversations
Scattered all over this road in Mystic, Connecticut,
That taste good nevertheless, and are bad for you.

A Sudden Rain in the Green Mountains

for Jessica Bennett

Plush hills, the raw materials, fall away.
The soaking clay
In which the serried oaks, the picturesque
And swaybacked pines, elected to evolve,
The famous marble in its bare reserve,

Vanish like guesses in these verticals
Whose heft at dusk
Blurs rooks to ridges, veils the bicycles
And splashes where they lean hard into curves.
Looming like crowds, such weather makes its world;

Its crash and draft and spate and uniform
Consonant force confirm
Or mean – not that without you there are no
Attainments I can care for or call good –
But that among them, missing you, I know
How much delight, green need

And weird vivacious luck drew me to you:
Luck lasts with us. Out here I can believe
That all companionships only rehearse
Or faintly copy ours, and make it plain –
As over the plain inn, the plain roof clears –
That granite, marble, nascent evening stars
And that impressive dinner bell, the moon,

Still seem – may seem, to me, forever – yours,
A portraitist's surround to set you off
For admiration and comparison.
In light you spare, unevenly, they shine
To give such thought, your thought, occasion,
Triangulate, and show me where you are.
I'm not with you. I will be with you soon.

SLOAN
0777 444 8132
Scrap Business

Childwall

Sways